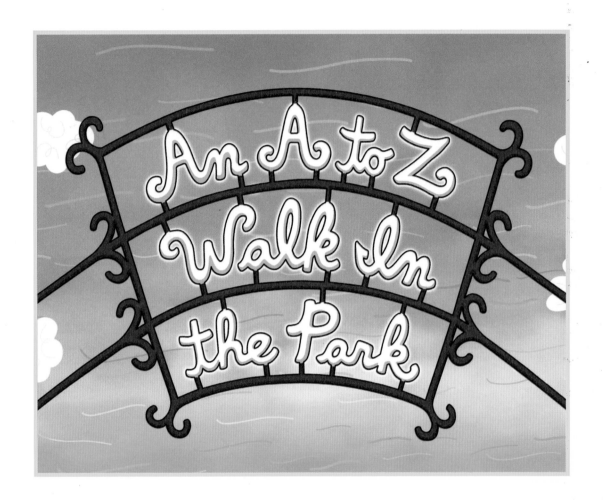

by R. M. Smith

Clarence-Henry Books • Alexandria, VA

An A to Z Walk In the Park
by R. M. Smith

Clarence-Henry Books • Alexandria, VA
Copyright © 2008 R. M. Smith

Design and Layout by R. M. Smith

Summary: Identify over 200 beasts in 26 letter descriptions as easy as a walk in the park.

Library of Congress Control Number: 2008902587

ISBN-10: 0-615-19572-5
ISBN-13: 978-0-615-19572-8

First Edition
10 9 8 7 6 5 4 3 2 1

Printed and bound in U.S.A.

www.atozwalk.com

To Mary, Phoebe, Luna, Chuka and the Fish

Footprints lead through an open gate upon
a path that winds into a park full of wild
and not so wild creatures from A to Z.

Ambling
about
the park
for the
letter

Aa

approaches
an Alligator
allying
with an
Aye-aye
and a
host of
affable
walk-alongs.

Aye-Aye

Ant

Antelope

Armadillo

Anteater

Aphid

Alligator

Blue Jay

Boa
Constrictor

Bat

Butterfly

Bear

Beetle

Baboon

Badger

Bee

Before long
bounds
the letter

Bb

which has
its own
batch
of friends
abuzz
such as
Butterflies,
a Baboon,
and a Bat.

Crazy not to
be outdone
the letter **Cc** creeps with it's own cluster of creatures
including a **Chimp** on a **Camel**, and a
Calico Cat keeping guard.

Caterpillar

Chimp

Cheetah

Cardinal

Camel

Calico Cat

Cicada

Cobra

Chipmunk

Cricket

Dragonfly

Dingo

Dove

Donkey

Duck

Dalmatian

Deer

Darter

Hee-hawin' and clip-cloppin' down the path for the letter

Dd

comes a Donkey joined by a Deer and a spotted Dalmatian.

Once the
Donkey had
hee-hawed
his goodbye
the letter

Ee

enters with an
eyeful of
Elephant
and an
edgy Emu.

Eagle

Elephant

Egret

Emu

Earthworm

Ermine

Echidna

Earwig

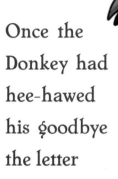

Flying Squirrel

Flamingos

Foxhound

Fish

Ferret

Frog

Firefly

Fox

Dropping in overhead, for the letter

Ff

flies in a Flying Squirrel, and just below peers a Fox, a Frog, and Fish swimming up stream.

Great it
is to be
the letter

Gg

with such
fine keepers of
this character
including
a giant Giraffe,
a beastly
Gorilla, and
a genial
Guinea Pig.

Greyhound

Gazelle

Gorilla

Grasshopper

Gold
Finch

Giraffe

Grouse

Ginea Pig

Garter Snake

Hinting that it might be their turn now, the beasts from

Hh

put forth a Horse, a hungry Hippopotamus, and a Hedgehog.

Hawk

Hyena

Hippopotamus

Horny Toad

Hermit Crab

Hare

Horse

Hedgehog

Imagine creatures under the guise of the letter

Ii

itching to be an Iguana, an Ibex, or perhaps an Irish Setter?

Indri

Ibis

Irish Setter

Iiwi

Impala

Inch Worm

Iguana

Ibex

Just as things started to settle down, up jumps the letter

Jj

juggling the stare of a Jaguar, and the grin of a happy Javelina.

Jaguarundi

Javelina

Jackal

Jackrabbit

Jerboa

June Bug

Jaguar

Kindly
keeping
pace
where "J"
left off

Kk

kicks in
with a
Kangaroo, a
Koala, and a
tail hugging
Kinkajou.

Kookaburra

Kinkajou

Kingfisher

Koala

Kangaroo

Kakapo

Komodo Dragon

Kiwi

Katydid

Lucky to lure in the king of the jungle, the letter

Ll

lucks out with a Lion, a Llama and a lounging Leopard.

Loris

Leopard

Lemur

Lynx

Llama

Lion

Lizard

Ladybug

Marching
merrily
upon the
middle ground

Mm

moves onto
the scene with
a mighty Moose,
a swimming
Manatee, and
a Monkey up
a tree.

Mocking-
bird

Monkey

Malamute

Meerkat

Markhor

Manx

Marten

Mongoose

Mallard

Mule

Moose

Muskrat

Manatee

Mudskipper

Moth

Milksnake

Niftily the letter **Nn** nets a Newt, and a Nuthatch.

On the wall for the letter **Oo** an Orangutan, an Oriole, and an Otter pose.

Owl

Okapi

Ostrich

Nuthatch

Newfoundland

Opossum

Ocelot

Otter

Orangutan

Newt

Oriole

Pigeon

Polar Bear

Pony

Puma

Platypus

Prairie Dog

Praying Mantis

Puffin

Pitta

Panda

Pacing down the path for the letter

Pp

parades a Panda, a Polar Bear as well as a Pony, Puma, and a Puffin.

The letter **Qq** is quick with a Quail and a Quetzal. **Rr** rallies with a Rhino, a Reindeer, and a Raccoon.

Raccoon

Quetzal

Reindeer

Quail

Rhinoceros

Ratel

Rattlesnake

Rooster

Swerving but steady the letter **Ss** sees that Snails and Sloths are slow and Sharks and Stingrays are speedy.

Sheep

Squirrel

Sloth

Snail

Skunk

Swans

St. Bernard

Seal

Shark

Salamander

Stingray

Starfish

Trotting through a canopy of trees the letter

Tt

tames a Toucan, Toad, and Turtle. The Tiger, on the other hand, is not tamed so easily.

Toucan

Thrush

Tarsier

Tamarin

Tanager

Tiger

Turtle

Toad

Tarantula

Tapir

Verdin

Uakari

Viceroy

Viper

Urial

Vicuna

Vizsla

Vole

Under
the
letter

Uu

the
unusual
Uakari
climbs and
the Urial
looks on.

Vying for
the letter

Vv

the Vizsla
and Vicuna
hold their
own.

Waiting in
the wild
without a
blink or
a wink
the letter

Ww

wells up
with a
Waterbuck,
Walrus,
and a
Wildebeest.

Woodpecker

Wren

Wooly Bear

Warthog

Waterbuck

Wombat

Weasel

Water Snake

For the letter **Xx** a Xenops stands sideways.

Yonder comes the letter **Yy** yielding a Yellow Lab, and a Yak!

Zebu

Zeren

Zebra
Butterfly

Zebra

Zorilla

Twenty-six
letters and
the alphabet
ends here
with the
letter

Zz

zooming
out with
three Zebras,
a Zorilla
and a Zebu.

Thanks for visiting An A to Z Walk In the Park!

Please come by again!

Index of animals in this book

Aa .... Alligator, Ant, Anteater, Antelope, Aphid, Armadillo, Aye-Aye

Bb .... Baboon, Badger, Bat, Bear, Beetle, Blue-jay, Boa Constrictor, Butterfly

Cc .... Calico Cat, Camel, Cardinal, Caterpillar, Cheetah, Chimp, Chipmunk, Cicada, Cobra, Cricket

Dd ... Dalmatian, Darter, Deer, Dingo, Donkey, Dove, Dragonfly, Duck

Ee .... Eagle, Earthworm, Earwig, Echidna, Egret, Elephant, Emu, Ermine

Ff ..... Ferret, Firefly, Fish, Flamingos, Flying Squirrel, Fox, Foxhound, Frog

Gg ... Garter Snake, Gazelle, Giraffe, Gold Finch, Gorilla, Grass Hopper, Greyhound, Grouse, Guinea Pig

Hh ... Hare, Hawk, Hedgehog, Hermit Crab, Hippopotamus, Horny Toad, Horse, Hyena

Ii ...... Ibex, Ibis, Iguana, Iiwi, Impala, Inch Worm, Indri, Irish Setter

Jj ...... Jackal, Jackrabbit, Jaguar, Jaguarundi, Javelina, Jerboa, June Bug

Kk ... Kakapo, Kangaroo, Katydid, Kingfisher, Kinkajou, Kiwi, Koala, Komodo Dragon, Kookaburra

Ll ..... Lady Bug, Lemur, Leopard, Lion, Lizard, Llama, Loris, Lynx

Mm .. Malamute, Mallard, Manatee, Manx, Markhor, Marten, Meerkat, Milksnake, Mockingbird, Mongoose, Monkey, Moose, Moth, Mudskipper, Mule, Muskrat

Nn ... Newfoundland, Newt, Nuthatch

Oo ... Ocelot, Okapi, Opossum, Orangutan, Oriole, Ostrich, Otter, Owl

Pp .... Panda, Pigeon, Pitta, Platypus, Polar Bear, Pony, Prairie Dog, Praying Mantis, Puffin, Puma

Qq ... Quail, Quetzal

Rr .... Raccoon, Ratel, Rattlesnake, Reindeer, Rhino, Rooster

Ss ..... Salamander, Seal, Shark, Sheep, Skunk, Sloth, Snail, Squirrel, St. Bernard, Starfish, Stingray, Swan

Tt ..... Tamarin, Tanager, Tapir, Tarantula, Tarsier, Thrush, Tiger, Toad, Toucan, Turtle

Uu ... Uakari, Urial

Vv .... Verdin, Viceroy, Vicuna, Viper, Vizsla, Vole

Ww .. Walking Stick, Wallaby, Walrus, Wapiti, Warthog, Wasp, Waterbuck, Water Snake, Weasel, Weevil, Whooping Crane, Wildebeest, Wolf, Wombat, Woodpecker, Wooly Bear, Wren

Xx .... Xenops, Xerus

Yy .... Yak, Yapok, Yellow Lab, Yuma Skipper

Zz .... Zebra, Zebra Butterfly, Zebu, Zeren, Zorilla